AVAILABLE NOW
from Lerner Publishing Services!

The *On the Hardwood* series:

Atlanta Hawks
Boston Celtics
Brooklyn Nets
Chicago Bulls
Charlotte Hornets
Cleveland Cavaliers
Dallas Mavericks
Denver Nuggets
Detroit Pistons
Golden State Warriors

Houston Rockets
Indiana Pacers
Los Angeles Clippers
Los Angeles Lakers
Miami Heat
Milwaukee Bucks
Memphis Grizzlies
Minnesota Timberwolves
New Orleans Pelicans
New York Knicks

Oklahoma City Thunder
Orlando Magic
Philadelphia 76ers
Phoenix Suns
Portland Trail Blazers
Sacramento Kings
San Antonio Spurs
Toronto Raptors
Utah Jazz
Washington Wizards

To Order • www.lernerbooks.com • 800-328-4929 • fax 800-332-1132

ON THE HARDWOOD

J.M. SKOGEN

On the Hardwood: Toronto Raptors

MVP Books
2255 Calle Clara
La Jolla, CA 92037

MVP Books is an imprint of Book Buddy Digital Media, Inc., 42982 Osgood Road, Fremont, CA 94539

MVP Books publications may be purchased for
educational, business, or sales promotional use.

Cover and layout design by Jana Ramsay
Copyedited by Susan Sylvia & Renae Reed
Photos by Getty Images

ISBN: 978-1-62920-176-4 (Library Binding)
ISBN: 978-1-62920-177-1 (Soft Cover)
ISBN: 978-1-62920-174-0 (eBook)

TABLE OF CONTENTS

Chapter 1
Oh, Canada

When people think about sports in Canada, basketball is not usually the first thing that comes to mind. Cold weather sports like hockey and curling are more iconic Canadian pastimes. However, many NBA fans would be surprised to learn how firmly basketball's roots are planted north of the U.S. border.

James Naismith, the man who invented basketball, was born in what is now the province of Ontario, Canada. He moved to the U.S. as an adult, but never forgot his Canadian heritage. In 1891, Naismith was a P.E. teacher in Massachusetts, where the winters were long and cold—much like they are in many parts of Canada. Naismith wanted to create a new sport for students to play inside when the weather made outside sports

more difficult. He studied many different sports, including hockey and another Canadian favorite— lacrosse—before coming up with

Dr. James Naismith poses with his first basketball team in Springfield, Massachusetts.

"Basket Ball." By 1893, the new sport was such a hit that children across the U.S. were all playing basketball at their local YMCAs.

Many years later, when the Basketball Association of America (BAA) was established in 1946, the first game was played in Canada. On November 1, 1946, the Toronto Huskies took on the New York Knickerbockers at Toronto's Maple Leaf Gardens. Some people consider this to be the first game in National Basketball Association (NBA) history as well, since the BAA went on to become the NBA. Unfortunately for the Huskies, their franchise folded after one less-than-stellar season, and professional basketball was absent from Canada for 50 years.

By the early 1990s, many people—both in Canada and the U.S.—thought that it was time for the NBA to expand into Canada. Toronto, Ontario, in particular, was

Toronto's skyline, overlooking Lake Ontario.

quick to throw its hat into the ring for a new NBA franchise. Usually a city has one bid group that tries to convince the NBA to expand into their city. In Toronto's case, three different bid groups tried to get the NBA's attention. There was no doubt that there was demand for basketball in Toronto—it quickly just became a question of the terms. Toronto and the NBA both wanted a new franchise to be successful, and one bid group in particular found a way to make sure that would happen. The winning bidders proposed a new, downtown arena that would be built near a subway line. This would make it easy

Shortly before the start of the Raptors' first season, Toronto's SkyDome hosted the 1994 FIBA World Championships.

for fans to get to the games, even in the dead of winter.

In 1993, it was announced that Toronto would be one of two Canadian cities to have an expansion team for the 1995-96 season. The other city was Vancouver, British

voted on a name, there was a distinct dinosaur preference among the entries. This was because the 1993 movie *Jurassic Park* had taken the world by storm. It was impossible to think of a bigger, meaner or fiercer creature than a prehistoric reptile. In the end, the most popular name was the "Raptors"— which was short for "velociraptor." Anyone who has seen *Jurassic Park* will remember those cunning, smart, deadly dinosaurs. They were not as big as the more famous T. rex, but they hunted in packs, and used clever strategies to take down their prey.

On May 15, 1994, the Toronto Raptors' new name and logo was

Columbia—which is a province on the west coast of Canada. Though Toronto is closer to the East Coast, near Buffalo, New York, they originally played in the Central Division.

Some people in Toronto wanted to name the new NBA franchise the "Huskies," in honor of their old BAA franchise. However, when the public

announced as "the newest, freshest, and hungriest look in the NBA." Their logo featured a huge, red raptor dribbling a basketball—with long claws, and an open mouth full of sharp teeth. The new team colors were a vivid red, purple, black, and a silver that was dubbed "Naismith Silver" in honor of the Canadian inventor of the game.

Like most expansion franchises, the Raptors were not immediately successful. There are many reasons for this. First, it can take a while for players and coaches to all get used to each other and gel as a team. Second, it can take expansion teams a little

International Draft Day
To help promote basketball in Canada, the 1995 NBA Draft was held in Toronto.

longer to lure really great players to their team.

In theory, the NBA takes many steps so that a new franchise will start out on equal footing with the rest

Isiah Thomas, Toronto's first general manager, bursts through the Raptors' logo.

11

Carlos Rogers takes off for a slam dunk during the Raptors' first season.

of the League. The NBA expansion draft is one of these measures. In an expansion draft, older franchises can choose certain players to protect, but the rest can be selected by a new team to help fill their roster. This does not mean, however, that players who are drafted by a new team will want to play for that team. The Raptors had the first pick in the 1995 Expansion Draft, and used that pick to choose the Chicago Bulls' point guard, B. J. Armstrong. Armstrong, however, did not want to play for Toronto, and refused to report for training camp. This forced the Raptors to immediately trade him away to the Golden State Warriors.

After the expansion draft, the new Canadian teams had another chance to acquire new players in

Damon Stoudamire shoots against the Atlanta Hawks during a preseason game.

the regular NBA Draft. Toronto's first pick in the 1995 NBA Draft was 5'10" Damon Stoudamire. At first, Toronto fans were not happy with this choice. They wanted someone who looked more imposing. Stoudamire was short compared to many NBA greats, and didn't really look like he had "star quality." However, Stoudamire soon showed Toronto, and all of the NBA, how much he was worth. Toronto fans started calling their star "Mighty Mouse" because of his strength compared to his size, and also because he had a tattoo of the cartoon "Mighty Mouse" on his arm. After setting the record for most 3-pointers by a rookie (133), Stoudamire took home the 1996 Rookie of the Year award.

Chapter 2
VINSANITY

The Toronto Raptors struggled during their first few seasons, not just to win games, but to create an identity in the League and in their home city. As one of only two teams north of the U.S. border, it was all too easy to feel overlooked by the rest of the NBA. By 1997-98, the Raptors had yet to make their mark in a lasting way. The novelty of their new franchise was wearing off, and they had never advanced to the playoffs, or even posted a winning regular season record.

This slow start was normal for most expansion teams—the Vancouver Grizzlies were also having a rough beginning—but it was very discouraging for fans. Attendance at the SkyDome had dipped from third in the League during their first season (950,330), to 16th in their third season (674,685).

Toronto was also without its first star. The Raptors, hoping to improve their roster with some fresh blood on the court, dealt "Mighty Mouse" Damon Stoudamire to the Portland Trail Blazers in the middle of the 1997-98 season. This trade did not

The Raptors' mascot entertains the crowd at the SkyDome in 1997.

When he was drafted in 1997, Tracy McGrady was ready to be Toronto's next star.

they hoped that his youthful potential would help breathe new life into their franchise. The 6'8" phenom had been named High School Player of the Year by *USA Today*, and took home the Most Valuable Player award in the Adidas ABCD Camp. All of this national attention made McGrady impatient to enter the professional world. He chose to skip college, and go directly from high school to the NBA. At 18 years old, McGrady was the youngest player in the League at the start of his rookie season.

Unfortunately, it took McGrady a little while to adjust to life in the NBA. After living most of his life in Florida, Canada was a completely different experience. McGrady also didn't really

prove to be a quick fix, and the 1997-98 season ended with a franchise-worst 16-66 record.

What Toronto fans craved was a new, exciting leader who would put Toronto on the map. Many people thought that star might be shooting guard Tracy McGrady. When Toronto chose McGrady with the No. 9 pick in the 1997 NBA Draft,

know anyone in Toronto beyond his teammates, and ended up spending a lot of time alone. Possibly due to his rookie status, coach Darrell Walker only played McGrady an average of 13 minutes per game. As McGrady searched for his identity and playing time, Toronto was still left searching for a star. Luckily, they didn't have long to wait.

At the start of the 1998-99 season, the Raptors traded their No. 4 pick in the 1998 NBA Draft, Antawn Jamison, to the Golden State Warriors for their No. 5 pick, Vince Carter. Carter, it turned out, had quite a bit in common with McGrady. They were both from Florida, and they both could play either shooting guard or small forward. They also happened to be cousins. The relationship was distant, and by marriage, but McGrady was still thrilled when he learned that Carter would soon be moving to Toronto.

Carter and McGrady were fast

Vince Carter and Antawn Jamison exchange hats, and teams, during the 1998 NBA Draft.

friends, and great teammates. Other Raptors commented that Carter and McGrady weren't just cousins—they were more like twins. They spent all their free time together, and even chatted to each other via cell phones if they were seated at different ends of the team bus. Together, the cousins helped to raise the level of the Raptors' game, and their own. By the end of the 1998-99 lockout shortened season, Toronto had posted a much improved 23-27 record. Though not yet a winning record, this percentage was by far Toronto's best. Vince Carter also managed to snag the 1999 NBA Rookie of the Year Award.

But it wasn't until the middle of the 1999-2000 season that the Raptors launched themselves into

Vince Carter and Tracy McGrady were cousins, friends, and teammates.

the NBA's spotlight. During the NBA All-Star Weekend, Vince Carter dazzled the world at the Slam Dunk Contest. When Vince Carter stepped onto the court, spectators had no idea that they were about to witness a groundbreaking performance.

Carter's leaps and spins were unlike anything the audience had ever seen. He astonished the crowd with his "360 windmill flush," where he spun around in mid-air before slamming one home. Another trick found Carter hanging from the net by the crook of his elbow—leaving fans crying out in surprise. Carter later said of his tricks, "I looked like I'd done it before, but inside I was like, 'Whew, I'm glad that worked.'" Carter blew every-

Vince Carter shows off his amazing moves at the 2000 All-Star Slam Dunk Contest.

one else out of the water, and easily took home the trophy.

After that day, everyone knew

Tasty Names

Carter's slam dunk trick, where he hung from the rim by his elbow, was called the "honey dip" or the "cookie jar" dunk.

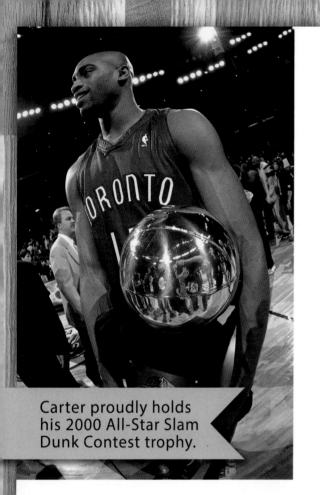

hang his poster on their walls.

The 1999-2000 season just kept getting better. First of all, this was the first full season that the Raptors played in Air Canada Centre—a brand-new arena that the Raptors shared with the National Hockey League's Toronto Maple Leafs. Also, after Carter's epic slam dunk performance, many people around Toronto who were not previously basketball fans came out to fill Air Canada Centre's seats, and to witness Carter take flight.

who Vince Carter was, and what jersey he proudly wore. When anyone in the NBA heard the words "slam dunk" they immediately thought of Carter. Fans in both Canada and the U.S. came down with a bad case of "Vinsanity" and flocked to buy Carter's jersey, and made room to

After posting a franchise-best 45-37 regular season record in 1999-2000, the Raptors reached the playoffs for the first time. The Raptors team, which included McGrady and Carter in the backcourt, and veterans Charles Oakley and Antonio Davis in the frontcourt, was a force to be reckoned with. Many fans wondered how far their beloved team would go. Unfortunately, Toronto was swept by the veteran New York Knicks, and didn't advance past the first round. However, just making it into the postseason was a triumph, and Toronto fans were convinced that their team had finally turned over a new leaf.

When Tracy McGrady became a free agent after the 1999-2000 season, he decided to step out of his cousin's shadow. He left Toronto and moved back to Florida to play for the Orlando Magic. Some fans were worried what this would mean for the momentum of their

Long Time No See
The 2000 Slam Dunk Contest marked the return of the event, after a two-year break.

team. However, the fans in Canada continued to believe in Carter, who had swiftly become the new face of their franchise.

Antonio Davis dunks against the Knicks during the first round of the 2000 NBA Playoffs.

21

Chapter 3
BATTLE FOR THE EAST

Vince Carter entered the 2000-01 season with a shiny new gold medal, having helped Team USA win first place in the 2000 Olympics. Fans took to calling Carter "Air Canada" (a play on their new arena, and Carter's leaping ability), "Vinsanity," and "Half-Man, Half-Amazing." Those same fans thought that this could be the breakout year for the Raptors. This belief was only made stronger when, after tallying a franchise-best 47-35 regular season record, the Raptors went head-to-head with the Knicks once again in the postseason.

This time, instead of being swept by the older team, the Raptors more than held their own. Toronto emerged

as victors, winning the series in five games. After their crucial first round victory, Vince Carter said, "The monkey is off our back. We're moving

Vince Carter and his Olympic teammate, Kevin Garnett, show off their gold medals.

23

Hanging Out

Air Canada Centre is also known as "the Hangar." A hangar is a large building used for storing airplanes.

on to bigger and better things."

The win against the Knicks not only marked the first time that the Raptors had advanced to the Eastern Conference Semifinals, but also the first postseason series victory for a Canadian NBA team. Indeed, the Raptors' expansion-mate, the Vancouver Grizzlies, had yet to post a winning season at all. By the 2001-02 season, the Grizzlies would pack up their bags and head to Memphis, Tennessee, leaving the Raptors as the only NBA team representing the entire Canadian nation.

Up next in the Eastern Conference Semifinals were the Philadelphia 76ers, led by superstar Allen Iverson. What followed was one of the greatest playoff duels in the history of the NBA. Carter and Iverson squared off like boxers in a ring,

The Philadelphia 76ers' Allen Iverson posed the biggest threat for the Raptors.

24

Carter and Iverson were the stars of the 2001 NBA Eastern Conference Semifinals.

trading shots instead of punches. The two teams alternated wins for the first four games, with Carter and Iverson sometimes scoring in bunches. For example, in Game 3, when Toronto won 102-78, Carter put up 50 of his team's points. Raptors fans were on the edges of their seats during the series, and people who weren't fans of either team tuned in for the sheer excitement that the two superstars provided.

When the 76ers managed to win Games 4 and 5, it was up to the Raptors to secure a Game 6 victory if they wanted to push the series to

The 76ers look on as the Raptors win Game 6.

the 76ers, they had to stop Iverson. In the 76ers' Game 5 victory, Iverson scored 52. The Raptors' solution was to throw more people at Iverson in Game 6, double-teaming him at all times. By halftime of Game 6, it was clear their new strategy was working—Iverson only had scored six points, and the Raptors led 54-39.

Early in the fourth quarter, the 76ers rallied and only trailed by two. However, Vince Carter started sinking everything he threw at the rim, and the Raptors survived, 101-89. At the end of the game, it was clear that the whole Toronto team had contributed to this victory.

a deciding Game 7. By then, Toronto had figured out that in order to stop

Perfect Attendance

From 2002 to 2006, Morris Peterson played in 370 straight regular season games. This was a team record.

Antonio Davis and rookie Morris Peterson both played a fantastic game, scoring 17 points each. Carter had another monster game, tallying an impressive 39 points.

Game 7 took place on May 20, 2001 in Philadelphia. For the 76ers, a win would mean the end of a 16-year absence from the Eastern Conference Finals. For the Raptors, it was a chance to prove that they belonged at the top of the NBA, a first for their city and home country.

For Vince Carter, May 20th meant something else entirely: It was his graduation day. When he left college during his junior year to play in the NBA, Carter had promised his mother that he would graduate. After continuing his education while in the NBA, Carter was finally going to receive

Toronto's Antonio Davis blocks a shot during the 2001 NBA Eastern Conference Semifinals.

27

his diploma. Carter graduated in the morning in North Carolina, and flew back to Philadelphia with plenty of time to get ready for the game. However, some people still questioned if traveling on game day was the best choice. With so much riding on Game 7, fans didn't want anything else on their star's mind.

Game 7 was a tight one. Toronto trailed 88-87 with possession of the ball, with only a few seconds to play. There was just enough time to inbound the ball to Carter, who launched a desperate arcing shot toward the basket as the buzzer sounded. The ball bounced off the rim, and into history. It was a missed

Vince Carter drives past the 76ers' Aaron McKie. Game 7 of the 2001 NBA Eastern Conference Semifinals was a battle for both teams.

shot that Raptors fans would never forget. The 76ers would advance to the Eastern Conference Finals, and the Raptors were sent home.

Many people later criticized Carter for the shot, and said that he shouldn't have attended his graduation that morning. In an interview 13 years later, however, Carter maintained that he had no regrets about being there in person to receive his degree: "That was a monumental moment in my career, personally and as a professional player. I was able to accomplish two of my goals: to make it deep into the playoffs,

and to graduate. So that day is something I will never forget and always cherish."

GREAT SERIES! YOU'RE NOT JUST A HOCKEY TOWN ANYMORE

A Philadelphia 76ers fan shows appreciation for the Raptors after Game 7.

Chapter 4
A NEW STAR

After the Raptors' inspiring 2000-01 season, Toronto fans couldn't wait to see what the next year would bring. To keep their winning team together, the Raptors agreed to a six-year contract extension with Vince Carter, and re-signed power forward/center Antonio Davis. They also added star Hakeem "the Dream" Olajuwon to the roster.

Olajuwon had led the Houston Rockets to the 1994 and 1995 NBA titles, and was in the top 10 all-time in points, blocks, steals, and rebounds. The veteran player was 38 years old, and he needed to ice his knees more often than when he was younger. But he still put up a respectable 16 points per game during the 2000-01 season. Toronto hoped that "the Dream's" championship experience

Going Greek

Antonio Davis was originally drafted by the Indiana Pacers in 1990. Davis, however, decided to play for the Greek League for two seasons, before eventually signing with the Pacers in 1993. Davis was traded to the Raptors in 1999.

would guide the Raptors to the top of the League in 2001-02.

Despite such high hopes for a championship run, the season that

Hakeem Olajuwon grabs a rebound during his single season with the Raptors.

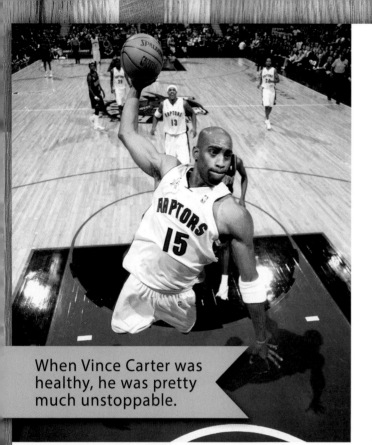

When Vince Carter was healthy, he was pretty much unstoppable.

the Detroit Pistons in five games, and a season that had started with so much potential came to an abrupt end. Olajuwon retired at the end of the season, without helping Toronto capture an NBA title.

In 2002-03, the Raptors recorded a dismal 24-58 regular season record—their worst since the 16-66 record in 1997-98. Though no fan wanted to sit through a losing season, the pain turned out to be worth it when Toronto collected the fourth pick in the 2003 NBA Draft. They used that pick to snag 6'11" Chris Bosh. The fact that Chris Bosh wasn't snatched up before the Raptors' No. 4 pick is a reflection of the strength of his draft

unfolded was pretty average. While Toronto did post a winning record and advance to the playoffs—a feat that would have thrilled Raptors fans just a few years earlier—they were missing a key player. Vince Carter had battled injury all season, and sat out the entire postseason. In the opening round, Toronto was dispatched by

class, which included LeBron James, Carmelo Anthony, and Dwyane Wade. After the draft, many NBA teams approached the Raptors wanting to trade for Bosh, but all offers were firmly turned down. Toronto wanted their franchise to keep improving, and they needed strong, young players who could grow with them.

As a child, Bosh was always the tallest kid in the class, something that can be tough when you are in elementary school. When interviewed years later, Bosh explained: "You're not really tall but you're taller than everybody else, you know? Being like 5'6", you're the monster." Bosh found inspiration from

Chris Bosh poses before the 2003 NBA Draft.

From Hoops to Heroes

Not only is Chris Bosh a talented NBA player, but he is also a voice actor. Bosh plays a character in the superhero cartoon Marvel's *Hulk and the Agents of S.M.A.S.H.*

tall and thin basketball players like Kevin Garnett, because it showed that people who looked like him could make it in the NBA. In high school Bosh led his team to a state title, and won many honors including High School Player of the Year by Basketball America. He was also named "Mr. Basketball" by the Texas Association of Basketball Coaches.

Bosh then attended Georgia Tech and enjoyed great success right away. He was one of only two freshmen to lead the Atlantic Coast Conference in

Chris Bosh drives past Kevin Garnett of the Minnesota Timberwolves for an easy layup.

field goal percentage. Having always been an excellent student in high school, Bosh initially intended to complete his college education and graduate with a degree in graphic design. However, his overwhelming talent for the game could not be ignored. After his freshman year at Georgia Tech, Bosh entered the NBA Draft.

In his first season in Toronto, Bosh tallied 11.5 points and 7.4 rebounds per game—setting a new franchise record for most rebounds as a rookie. During several underwhelming seasons, in which the Raptors were absent from the postseason entirely, watching Chris Bosh's moves on the court was a highlight for fans. Though Vince Carter continued to play at a masterful level, he was often

Toronto fans show their love for their new star, Chris Bosh.

sidelined due to injury. Bosh swiftly became one of the most important players in Toronto.

Then, in the middle of the 2004-05 season, Carter was traded to the New Jersey Nets. "The Trade," as it came to be known, followed some disagreements between Carter

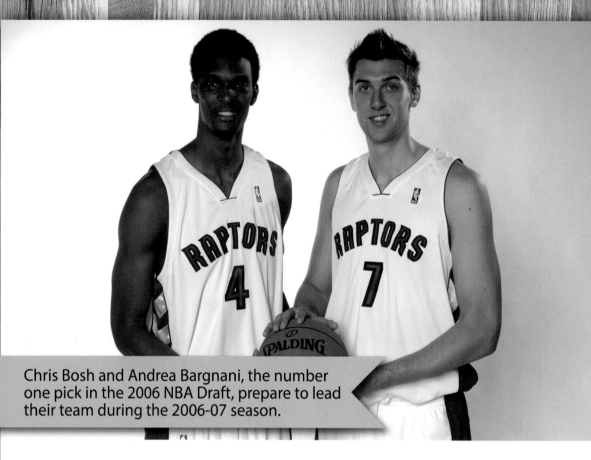

Chris Bosh and Andrea Bargnani, the number one pick in the 2006 NBA Draft, prepare to lead their team during the 2006-07 season.

and Raptors management. Toronto fans felt hurt, and even betrayed by Carter's departure. The Raptors received some promising players, and two first-round picks in exchange for Carter, but this did little to comfort the city. Fans did not appreciate the trend of young players leaving in their prime to play in other cities.

Lacking their first superstar, Toronto looked to Chris Bosh to become their new leader—a role he happily filled. In the summer of 2006, Bosh showed his commitment to the Raptors by signing a three-year contract extension. When Bosh announced his new contract with the Raptors, he also donated $1 million to a local Toronto charity called Community Legacy Projects.

With Bosh locked up for several more seasons in Toronto, the Raptors made a few more savvy moves to improve their roster. One of their biggest additions was the No. 1 pick in the 2006 NBA Draft, Italian-born Andrea Bargnani. Seven foot tall Bargnani was only the fourth NBA player to arrive from Italy, where he had been named the 2005-06 Euroleague Rising Star. Helping out Bosh and Bargnani on the court were point guard T.J. Ford and shooting guard Anthony Parker, who formed the core of the Raptors' 2006-07 team.

With 47 wins and 35 losses, 2006-07 marked the Raptors' first winning season in four years, and their best season since the unforgettable

Spitting Image

At a home game on January 7, 2007, the Toronto Raptors gave away 10,000 Andrea Bargnani figurines.

2000-01 trip to the Eastern Conference Semifinals.

When the Raptors lost to Vince Carter's Nets in the first round of the playoffs, it was a huge disappointment for fans. However, they knew that their team was heading in the right direction. The NBA community also acknowledged the positive steps that Toronto was taking as a franchise. The Raptors' coach, Sam Mitchell, took home the 2007 NBA Coach of the Year, and Toronto's president and general manager, Bryan Colangelo, was named NBA Executive of the Year.

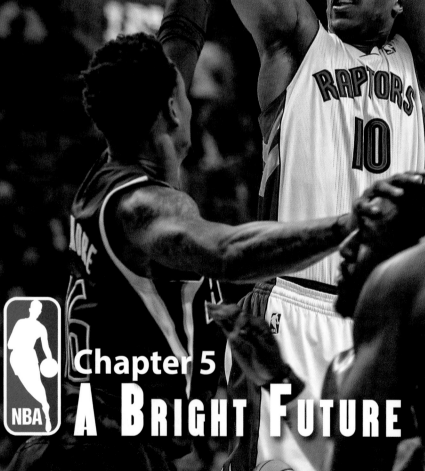

Chapter 5
A Bright Future

By the middle of the 2013-14 season, the Toronto Raptors had surprised most of the NBA by doing one simple thing: winning. In the fall, sports critics had labeled 2013-14 as another rebuilding season for the Raptors. It had been five years since the Raptors were real contenders in the NBA, and Toronto fans were thrilled by their team's sudden—and unexpected—improvement.

Rudy Gay, who joined the Raptors in January 2013, was supposed to be Toronto's next big star.

The last time that the Toronto Raptors had posted a winning season was 2007-08. A swift first-round exit in the postseason, however, ended a fairly successful era for the Raptors. Then, just after the 2009-10 season, the Raptors traded Chris Bosh to the Miami Heat. Bosh joined fellow 2004 draftees Dwyane Wade and LeBron James on the Heat's roster, and Toronto received two first-round draft picks as compensation. "We are certainly sorry to see Chris leave,"

Toronto Rapper

In 2013, the Raptors welcomed rapper Drake as the team's global ambassador. Drake was born in Toronto, and is a longtime fan of the team.

Bryan Colangelo said at the time, "but we are planning to use these acquired assets to retool our roster and evolve as an organization."

From 2007 to 2013, the Raptors tried many different things to restructure their roster and improve the team. They tried forming their team around Andrea Bargnani after the Chris Bosh trade, but that wasn't an immediate fix. They attempted to persuade veteran free agents, like Canadian Steve Nash, to join the team. Nash signed with the Los Angeles Lakers instead. Toronto also tried trading for big stars—bringing in Rudy Gay, for example, from the Memphis Grizzlies in January 2013. The Raptors also hoped that new prospects chosen in the NBA Draft would develop into key team members. Jonas Valančiūnas and Terrence Ross (the Raptors' 2011 and 2012 first-round draft picks) were

Andrea Bargnani soars to the basket against the Orlando Magic in 2010.

solid players, but did not instantly change the fate of the team.

By the end of the 2012-13 season, the Raptors were ready for some more basic changes to their franchise. They hired a brand new general manager, Masai Ujiri, who had big plans for his team. Ujiri was born in Nigeria, where his love of basketball grew through outdoor pickup games with friends, old basketball movies on VHS, and copies of Sports Illustrated. He was a fan of Hakeem Olajuwon, who was also from Nigeria. Eventually, Ujiri moved to the U.S. to pursue college hoops in North Dakota, before playing professionally in Europe for six years.

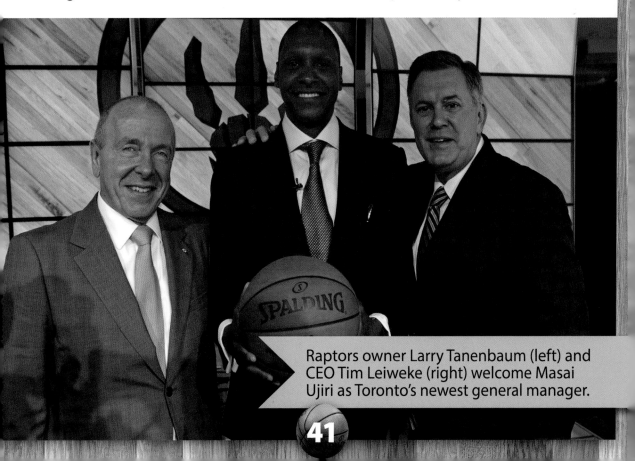

Raptors owner Larry Tanenbaum (left) and CEO Tim Leiweke (right) welcome Masai Ujiri as Toronto's newest general manager.

When he retired from professional basketball in 2002, Ujiri worked his way up the NBA management ladder, serving first as an international scout, then as assistant general manager for the Toronto Raptors. In 2010, Ujiri became the general manager for the Denver Nuggets—making him the first African-born GM in the NBA.

After helping the Nuggets to a 57-25 regular season record in 2012-13, Ujiri was named the NBA Executive of the Year. Ujiri was the first person who wasn't born in America to receive this honor.

After accepting the position of general manager for the Raptors in 2013, Ujiri immediately went to work.

Ujiri accepts his 2013 NBA Executive of the Year award.

First, he shook up the roster with big trades, trying to clear out some of the higher salaries in favor of young players with lots of potential. He traded away Andrea Bargnani to the New York Knicks. Then, in December, Ujiri made another drastic move and traded away star Rudy Gay to the Sacramento Kings. Gay had a huge salary, and freeing up that money would allow the Raptors to bolster their roster with more up-and-coming players.

Terrence Ross shoots over his old teammate, Rudy Gay, of the Sacramento Kings.

Many Toronto fans expected this roster move to pay out over several years, after the new team had time to gel. No one expected a 180-degree turnaround to occur so rapidly. It felt like Toronto had suddenly flipped a switch. Players started to click and, more impressively, win. In their first 20 games of the season (just before the Rudy Gay trade), Toronto's record

Priceless Experience

Ujiri's first "job" in the NBA was as an unpaid international scout for the Orlando Magic.

Toronto's DeMar DeRozan takes flight during a 2014 game against the Washington Wizards.

was 7-13. After the trade, they won 13 out of their next 20 games to draw even at 20-20.

One of the Raptors players who helped form the new core of the 2013-14 team was shooting guard DeMar DeRozan. Growing up in Compton, California, DeRozan avoided the widespread violence in his neighborhood by focusing on athletic success. DeRozan had been a key member of the Compton High School varsity basketball team since he was a freshman. In 2008, he ranked as the third best college recruit by

High Scorer

On January 22, 2014, DeRozan scored a career high 40 points in a game against the Dallas Mavericks.

Rivals.com. In his first season at the University of Southern California (USC), DeRozan was named Pac-10 Tournament MVP.

After just one year at USC, DeRozan decided to enter the 2009 NBA Draft. Though DeRozan was ready for a professional career, he wasn't only thinking about his game when he chose to leave school. His mother suffered from lupus, and a multi-million dollar contract would allow him to give her the best medical care available.

Though DeRozan didn't exactly hit the ground running as a rookie, he quickly improved and has led Toronto in scoring since the 2011-12 season. However, after taking on more of a leadership role after the Bargnani and Gay trades, DeRozan's already respectable 18.1 points per game in 2012-13 increased to 22.6 by March of 2013-14. As a result of

DeMar DeRozan first wore the No. 10 jersey at USC, and again as a Toronto Raptor.

Kyle Lowry drives to the basket during his first season in a Raptors' jersey.

his skyrocketing talent, DeRozan was selected to the 2014 All-Star team—making him the fourth Raptor to become an All-Star.

Helping DeRozan form one of the best backcourts in the League was point guard Kyle Lowry. When Lowry was traded to the Toronto Raptors in 2012, he had already been in the NBA for seven years—playing first for the Memphis Grizzlies, then for the Houston Rockets.

Lowry was always extremely driven to win—a trait that sometimes made it difficult for him to mesh well with teammates. However, it wasn't until the 2013-14 season that Lowry really stepped into the NBA's spotlight. After Ujiri's roster shuffles, Lowry's

Kyle Lowry, Terrence Ross, Jonas Valančiūnas, DeMar DeRozan, and Amir Johnson help form the new and improved 2013-14 Toronto Raptors.

playing time increased, and so did his scoring. His points per game jumped from 11.6 in 2012-13, to 16.8 as of March 2014. Toronto fans thought that Lowry should have been on the 2014 All-Star team alongside DeRozan.

The Raptors' fan base has stood by their team through success and disappointment. They will make sure the Raptors have all the support they need as they claw their way back to the postseason and, perhaps, to a long-awaited NBA Championship for their home city and supporting country. With new management, and an exciting roster, the Toronto Raptors are anything but "dinosaurs."